Miracle on Bourbon St.

Hurricane Katrina and the Relief of New Orleans

A Photo Memoir of the Largest Mass Rescue in US History

By Jim Bartlett

Printed in the United States of America

Second Printing, 2020

ISBN 978-1-7353222-1-6

Carentan Media Group
All Rights Reserved 2020

Dedication

This book is dedicated to my friend, teacher and mentor Kurt Schork, KIA Sierra Leone May 24th, 2000. His loss left a hole in my profession that can never be filled and is still deeply felt by all who knew him.

Acknowledgements

First, it must be said, my nephew, Isaac Anderson, was the best sidekick to have in the middle of all that. He had just turned sixteen and we headed out thinking this would just be another storm chase. It went completely sideways and he hung in there like a trooper. DMX "Bring Your Whole Crew" became our theme song. After it wrapped up and a security gig came on line for me, I put him on a Greyhound back to Virginia alone. He made it and started back in school the next week. He has gone on to do some extraordinary things since then.

The list also includes those who have inspired and encouraged, to include; Stu, Sam, Lorraine, Matty and the crew at www.UKWeatherworld.co.uk, Tom Cutler at USNI, Wade Goddard, Darko Bandic, LTC Patrick Fetterman, Col. Carl Bernard, Jim Nachtwey, Greg Marinovic, Corrine, Georgie, Hervoi, Corky, Jon & Eric, Samara, Deni & BJ, Ben, JS Mosby, Bob Brown, Tom, Cohiba Rob, Bailey, Mike, Karl & Mo, Nevada, Jay, Scott, Russ, the crew at Newsweek, Time & UPI, Jack Lawrence, Don North, Tobin Beck, the boys at 91st ENGs, Jeff Delacruz and the 425th CA, my Dad, Dennis and Dinah. There are many others, you know who you are.

Last, but most important; my sister Midge (thanks for letting me borrow your kid and taking care of Floyd), my Mother(s) and Julia. Without their unwavering support, I couldn't have done any of this over the years.

Many thanks are in order for the people of New Orleans, the Gulf Coast, and the first responders who went to their aid. Without them, this book wouldn't exist.

Prologue to the New Edition

I first wrote this over the winter of 2005-6, a few months after my return from NOLA. Of everything I have ever been through, NOLA was the most intense. After Bosnia, and Russia, Iraq, etc. that's saying something. It was undertaken in the spirit of catharsis and uploaded to one of the early print on demand sites. I printed off maybe six copies for family and then left it lay, moving onto other adventures.

But those days in NOLA have never strayed far from my memory, even more so than other places like Iraq or Bosnia. It's always been there, in the back of my mind, nearly every day. Now mind you it's not necessarily because it was such a tragic event. I've been party to those, especially the siege of Sarajevo, which was one of the worst injustices I have yet to witness.

It was more than that. It was the greatest coming together of people to save others and themselves I have ever been party to. When I tell my EMT students about it the energy returns in full. It was simply the most extraordinary thing I have ever been through. I have never seen so many people pull together, so intensely, in such a short period of time, in such a crazy place. Wildland fire comes close, but I don't think I'll ever see that again.

Recently I was tapped to help edit and produce a book for an old friend and it spurred me to go digging in old hard drives for Miracle on Bourbon St. Ver 1.0. I found it, and it was a digital mess. Just so you know, we've come a LONG way since 2005. But digging it out was the first step and now here it is.

I've trimmed a bit, added some, but by and large it's true to the original. The story I tell is still fresh, still relevant, like the memories that never faded. Here's to you NOLA. Love you forever.

Why I call it "Miracle on Bourbon St."

There will some who will take offense at the title of this book, "Miracle on Bourbon St." Many believe that the relief operation was anything but, echoing media accounts that "the pace of relief" was a "national disgrace," as Newsweek claimed. That couldn't be further from the truth. Despite an immediate rush to judgment and an outbreak of the blame game, the fact remains that hundreds of thousands were evacuated to locations where they had food, clean water and shelter in about a week. Considering the hand dealt to the rescue forces by this storm, that's not too bad. Bear in mind that none of the surrounding communities had even remotely prepared for a refugee influx of this size on such short notice.

You call 911, firemen come in minutes. With 90,000 square miles of declared disaster area, it wasn't going to be that simple. But help came and it started coming quickly, going up against some of the worst terrain mother nature could create. The mark of the professional is that they make the difficult look easy, perhaps too easy. So easy that we take it for granted.

Take the US Coast Guard's air rescue operations. The helicopter comes in, the rescue guy goes down on a wire, he puts people in the basket and when the chopper is full he goes back up on the wire and they fly away. Pretty straight forward one would think. Ah...not quite. When you see that Coast Guard or Para rescue guy go down on that wire on TV, you are watching an exceptionally dangerous endeavor that starts with the helicopter itself.

If you don't know much about them, picture an old time pocket watch, with all of its little gears and sprockets, powered by a jet engine and loaded with 2,000 gallons of rocket fuel. While waiting to go up in one of them, I had a chance to examine closely the cluster of five ¼ inch pins that keep the tail rotor attached to the gizmo thing that keeps the blades aligned properly. If one of those fails, the blades will start to oscillate wildly, shake themselves loose and send you for the Black Hawk Down, death spin into the ground maneuver.

Cool, but what now? Well, we're going to lower a guy down on this thin steel cable. It's small, but very strong, so strong in fact that if it gets hung up on something the chopper can become unstable and more or less spin itself out of the sky. The Black Hawk Down, tetherball crash and explode maneuver. When you're talking about something powered by a jet engine, you can loose control really, really quickly if this happens. There's a reason that it's easier to get to the cable cutter in the back of one of these things than it is to grab the fire extinguisher.

But not only are we going to lower some guy down on the end of this thing, we're going to lower him onto a building that is so damaged and so unstable that three months later a resident still cannot enter it because if they move one 2x4 the whole thing might fall over on them. And this is just one facet of the relief, just a helicopter hoist. Imagine coming alongside that same building in a fifteen foot Jon boat.

Essentially, the ground situation in New Orleans was perhaps the most difficult and dangerous urban search and rescue environment ever encountered in the United States.

If you want a comparable operation of the same scale, look at post Cindy Guatemala, where landslides buried entire villages killing thousands. They wound up simply placing large headstones where villages once stood. There was simply nothing they could do. So, do you see why I use the word "Miracle" in this context?

To have been part of this, to have struggled and worked alongside the people who pulled this off, it's a privilege and a source of pride I have a hard time describing. You all should be very, very proud of them. They're the best kind of people this country produces and we're damn lucky to have them around.

In any case, if you were down there, I hope you fared well, if not, my thoughts are with you.

Jim Bartlett

Katrina
Anatomy of Destruction

490
WWUS74 KLIX 281550
NPWLIX

URGENT - WEATHER MESSAGE
NATIONAL WEATHER SERVICE NEW ORLEANS LA
1011 AM CDT SUN AUG 28 2005

..DEVASTATING DAMAGE EXPECTED

HURRICANE KATRINA
A MOST POWERFUL HURRICANE WITH UNPRECEDENTED
STRENGTH...RIVALING THE INTENSITY OF HURRICANE CAMILLE OF 1969.

MOST OF THE AREA WILL BE UNINHABITABLE FOR WEEKS...PERHAPS LONGER.
AT LEAST ONE HALF OF WELL CONSTRUCTED HOMES WILL HAVE ROOF AND
WALL
FAILURE. ALL GABLED ROOFS WILL FAIL...LEAVING THOSE HOMES SEVERELY
DAMAGED OR DESTROYED.

THE MAJORITY OF INDUSTRIAL BUILDINGS WILL BECOME NON FUNCTIONAL.
PARTIAL TO COMPLETE WALL AND ROOF FAILURE IS EXPECTED. ALL WOOD
FRAMED LOW RISING APARTMENT BUILDINGS WILL BE DESTROYED.
CONCRETE BLOCK LOW RISE APARTMENTS WILL SUSTAIN MAJOR
DAMAGE...INCLUDING SOME WALL AND ROOF FAILURE.

HIGH RISE OFFICE AND APARTMENT BUILDINGS WILL SWAY
DANGEROUSLY...A FEW TO THE POINT OF TOTAL COLLAPSE. ALL WINDOWS
WILL BLOW OUT.

AIRBORNE DEBRIS WILL BE WIDESPREAD...AND MAY INCLUDE HEAVY ITEMS
SUCH AS HOUSEHOLD APPLIANCES AND EVEN LIGHT VEHICLES. SPORT
UTILITY VEHICLES AND LIGHT TRUCKS WILL BE MOVED. THE BLOWN DEBRIS
WILL CREATE ADDITIONAL DESTRUCTION. PERSONS...PETS...AND LIVESTOCK
EXPOSED TO THE
WINDS WILL FACE CERTAIN DEATH IF STRUCK.

POWER OUTAGES WILL LAST FOR WEEKS...AS MOST POWER POLES WILL BE
DOWN
AND TRANSFORMERS DESTROYED. WATER SHORTAGES WILL MAKE HUMAN
SUFFERING
INCREDIBLE BY MODERN STANDARDS.

THE VAST MAJORITY OF NATIVE TREES WILL BE SNAPPED OR UPROOTED.
ONLY
THE HEARTIEST WILL REMAIN STANDING...BUT BE TOTALLY DEFOLIATED. FEW
CROPS WILL REMAIN. LIVESTOCK LEFT EXPOSED TO THE WINDS WILL BE
KILLED.

AN INLAND HURRICANE WIND WARNING IS ISSUED WHEN SUSTAINED WINDS
NEAR
HURRICANE FORCE...OR FREQUENT GUSTS AT OR ABOVE HURRICANE
FORCE...ARE
CERTAIN WITHIN THE NEXT 12 TO 24 HOURS.

ONCE TROPICAL STORM AND HURRICANE FORCE WINDS ONSET...DO NOT
VENTURE
OUTSIDE!

MSZ080>082-282100-
HANCOCK-HARRISON-JACKSON-
1011 AM CDT SUN AUG 28 2005

POWER OUTAGES WILL LAST FOR WEEKS...AS MOST POWER POLES WILL BE
DOWN AND TRANSFORMERS DESTROYED. WATER SHORTAGES WILL MAKE
HUMAN SUFFERING INCREDIBLE BY MODERN STANDARDS.

THE VAST MAJORITY OF NATIVE TREES WILL BE SNAPPED OR UPROOTED.
ONLY THE HEARTIEST WILL REMAIN STANDING...BUT BE TOTALLY
DEFOLIATED. FEW
CROPS WILL REMAIN. LIVESTOCK LEFT EXPOSED TO THE WINDS WILL BE
KILLED.

AN INLAND HURRICANE WIND WARNING IS ISSUED WHEN SUSTAINED
WINDS NEAR HURRICANE FORCE...OR FREQUENT GUSTS AT OR ABOVE
HURRICANE FORCE...ARE
CERTAIN WITHIN THE NEXT 12 TO 24 HOURS.

ONCE TROPICAL STORM AND HURRICANE FORCE WINDS ONSET...DO NOT
VENTURE OUTSIDE!

MSZ080>082-282100-
HANCOCK-HARRISON-JACKSON-
1011 AM CDT SUN AUG 28 2005

"That is certainly the most worrying advisory I have ever read…"
Lorraine Evans, site administrator
UKWeatherworld.co.uk

"Everyone is talking wind, no one is talking surge. That's what is
going to kill a bunch of people. NWS is using "Catastrophic" to
describe this. You know how conservative they are with public
"Scare" words." Jim's post to UKWW an hour later.

My attempt to describe the indescribable.

Hurricane Katrina was one of the largest hurricanes in recent memory, it was certainly the largest storm I have ever chased. I am still staggered by the sheer size of it all these years later. It was simply a mega monster storm you had to see to believe.

For a week or so prior to its arrival, I had watched it slowly creep across the Atlantic with my storm chaser colleagues at www.UKWeatherworld.co.uk, the online MET site where I spend my weather time. Day after day it kept getting knocked down by wind shear, only to get back up in a matter of hours. I didn't expect it to survive and made no preparations to chase it. Having just returned from Hurricane Dennis, I was not eager to drive back to the Gulf Coast.

At the time, however, conditions in the Gulf of Mexico were about as good as it gets for major hurricane formation. Water temperatures were through the roof, there was no wind shear to speak of and any major meteorological formations, such as fronts or high pressure ridges, that could have had any effect were hundreds of miles away. As far as Gulf hurricanes go, this one was going to be "Perfect."

It initially hit Florida as a Category One and tracked westward into the Gulf. Moving slow, it just kept picking up steam until it was a CAT 5 of almost unbelievable scale. About this time Julia called me. She said, "Honey, where are you?" I said I was sitting at my desk at home and asked her why. "You need to look at the satellite imagery," she said. I pulled it up and saw that Katrina had spun up into the largest, most perfectly formed hurricane I had ever see. I started franticly packing the Jeep. Bless that girl.

At its height it was about the size of England, if one includes its feeder bands. The eye was 70 miles across and perfectly formed. On the morning of August 28th it set its sights on the Louisiana – Mississippi line and plowed north. As it came closer to Louisiana, its winds dropped a bit into the CAT 3-4 range, but it was still packing CAT 5 storm surge and that was what was going to be the killer.

Storm surge is when the air pressure at the core of a storm goes so low that the atmosphere can't hold the ocean down and hence the level of the sea rises beneath it. The spiral nature of the storm then spins that water into a column underneath it which creates this mass of water that will then ride up onto the shore. On top of that rise in sea level, the "Hurricane Force Winds" whip up mammoth waves. To make matters worse, Katrina was coming in on a morning high tide.

All afternoon on the 28th, it rained as feeder bands came onshore. At midnight on the 29th, it officially made landfall. By 06:00am it was pounding New Orleans and the Gulf Coast all the way to Mobile, AL. Very little on the coast stood a chance as the waters rose in many places to over 30 feet.

I find it hard to describe what happens when water in those quantities gets up with a head of surf on it. The force of this is something that has to be experienced to be believed. Water is huge. The sheer weight of waves is measured in tons. They smash into things like houses and break them up into match wood as if an avalanche has combined with an earthquake. They grab up all of the debris from that and continue to crash on shore, again and again for hours, a churning, crashing slurry of 2 x 4s, telephone poles, 2 x 8s, metal siding, automobiles, glass, everything. Imagine putting the aforementioned debris into a commercial washing machine and then climbing in. Have your friends start it up on the "Heavily soiled" setting. That's what happened to Mississippi.

At the same time that was going on, the hurricane dropped its other big killer…rain, tons of it, on a scale right out of the Bible. That, combined with the surge, is what filled Lake Ponchatrain and then, pushed by the wind into the canals, burst the levees in New Orleans. I mean, at this point, forget the wind. What the water is doing alone is bad enough.

But the wind won't be forgotten. Katrina threw gusts of over 100 mph. If you're not sure what that's like, try standing on top of your car while your spouse drives down the highway at 65 mph. It's the kind of wind that turns a street sign into a flying guillotine blade. It turns roofing nails and glass into bullets. There's a reason the prudent storm chaser wears a helmet.

But it gets worse. While the storm was kicking up sustained winds of 80 to 120 mph, an even more dangerous element was the tornadoes it spun off. Even minor tornadoes have winds that approach 200mph. If a twister grabs your Chevy Tahoe, it becomes a rock hurled by some petulant child having a tantrum. This storm is spinning them off by the dozen.

It's as if the Jolly Green Giant and all his buddies have been laid off from a steel mill and have gotten into a couple of cases of real bad whiskey. They're not so jolly now, and they've decided to smash up the mill town with golf clubs. Their rampage stretches from the coast up into Tennessee.

The storm itself hung together as a hurricane two thirds of the way into Mississippi and Alabama. It was only downgraded to a Tropical Depression (just a tick under Tropical Storm) near Clarkesville, TN. That's hundreds of miles from the Gulf Coast. It's unheard of in the world of hurricanes. Hurricanes don't do this. They hit land and break apart. Not this one, it came on like a freight train with nothing on gods earth to slow it down.

Miles and miles of roads were blocked by trees and power lines. Bridges were down, dikes have burst, debris has made residential streets unrecognizable. It went on and on for hundreds of miles. Your senses become overwhelmed by it after a while because it just doesn't end. I mean, from the coast south of Mobile all the way to Jefferson Parish, and halfway to Nashville, it's just smashed. I-10 East is blocked in a dozen places by washing machines, chunks of houses, fishing boats, and the forest. A major causeway into Biloxi is simply gone, nothing left but little concrete teeth sticking out of the water. Whole communities, such as Bay St. Louis, are no more than concrete slabs and there's a bazillion gallons of lake water rushing into downtown New Orleans.

That's what everybody had to get through. That's what everybody was up against to get in and get this rescue done. Thank god the I-10 was open west of NOLA and you can thank the National Guard and the Mississippi DOT guys for cutting their way in to the coast via I-10 East. And that's about it. Everything else was totally jacked up. Rural routes inland didn't get cleared for weeks.

Oh yea, and now there's hundreds of thousands of people who need to be rescued from the middle of it all and sent to somewhere safe.

I can only hope that I am conveying the magnitude of this event to you. It's still hard for me to grasp the enormity of it and I was there. I was on towards fifteen years of wars and disasters at that point and I've never seen anything like this, ever.

We were crouched behind a concrete column in downtown. Katrina's eye was coming onshore and we were catching serious wind. Only a strong CAT 1, but funneled through the urban valleys, cycloning, spinning shit up big time.

Down on Commerce St, there was a tall office building. It was sheathed by scaffolding that was host to hundreds of unsecured 2 x 6s. These, of course, started to come loose and fly through the air. One in particular caught my attention.

It was gently floating around, way up there, just lazily drifting and spinning. It looked as light as a feather…until it found its target and came soaring in like some kind of suicide drone. It was the most bizarre of things, for no apparent reason it just suddenly decided to come straight at us.

Just like in Little League, I kept my eye on the ball as it gained velocity, coming in as a blur. "Ready, ready and duck NOW!" KRA-BOOM! It struck the column we were hiding behind and smashed into pieces, flying past on both sides. A one in a million shot.

More pieces started to come loose as we dashed across a street to better shelter. It went on like that all day. An urban battlefield where the enemy was a super blob the size of god. We were nothing but rats, scurrying around under its wrath, surviving.

My buddy called on the cell phone. The roof of the Super Dome had peeled off and the levees had failed in three places. Shit was about to get as real as it gets.

And Now it Begins

After scurrying around under the storm we reset and headed towards the nearest airfield. There I managed to get onto a US Coast Guard rescue helicopter and spent a harrowing sixteen hour mission over the city. I had caught a brief glimpse of what was happening on the news in some lobby or something, but nothing prepared me for the magnitude of this disaster. Flying above it all, with a view that no camera can capture, was describable only as "complete" as far as the eye could see. The entire coastline was smashed. In some places it was just gone.

A day later we pushed back into the city and began work with the crews on the ground who were evacuating people by small boat. I encountered everyone from US Coastguardsmen from as far away as Iowa to a pair of swamp fishermen who brought in their shallow draft fishing boat, "The Nightstalker." They weren't alone. Boat owners from as far away as Taos, NM simply showed up, put in, and got busy. In many cases, when they became too exhausted to continue, they tossed the keys to total strangers so the boat could keep working.

I met firemen who on their own initiative had taken control of the situation at the University of New Orleans campus until forced to flee by gang violence. I encountered New Orleans policemen who stood their ground as best they could, despite the antiquity of their communications gear and overwhelming numbers of both victims and opportunists. I met policemen from distant rural departments who, without orders, took stock of what was happening on the news and just showed up on their own. I met ambulance crews and national guardsmen who found themselves pulling twenty hour days as they struggled to manage the exodus of people escaping the waters. In short, the New Orleans situation brought out thousands, civilian and professional alike, who just pushed in and made it happen.

I took all of this in, shooting, helping the crews, shooting some more. At the drop of a hat, the largest rescue operation in US history had been launched. Swarms of helicopters filled the sky, boats of every description plied the waters. This was taking place across a smashed and flooded landscape that presented every conceivable obstacle to rescuers. Most other places in the world, when hit with disasters of this magnitude, face weeks or months waiting for relief. This was up and moving, planned or otherwise, within hours. Abandonment of the city by its leadership didn't help much. The first FEMA teams on scene found the Emergency Operations Center deserted and locked. They flipped out tourist maps onto the hoods of their trucks and went to work anyway.

It was a privilege to document and serve alongside the workaday responders and citizens that answered the call, saddled up and shepherded tens of thousands to safety. They did a hell of a job in a very hard place to do it and everyone owes them a great deal.

Into the Fray. The Rescue of New Orleans

I'm waiting for the flight while a swarm of rotary and fixed wing aircraft comes and goes, round the clock, in and outbound for New Orleans and points along the Gulf Coast. Cocky young pilots and rescue swimmers who departed fresh faced and strutting, are returning hours and hours later, exhausted, looking like they've been pulled off a contested beachhead. Young mechanics go on working through the night to keep the birds just this side of mechanical failure. I find only a few hours of fitful sleep on the grass by the ramp, waiting for dawn.

The next morning an aircrew, who looks remarkably like the fresh ones from the night before, walks to the line and does their pre-flight brief. We're going to New Orleans.

Our helicopter is number 6013, from Clearwater, FL. She will serve us well this day. Her pilots, Lt. Brian Bailey and Lt. Michael Rasch, tick off a list of just about every hazard imaginable that could complicate a rescue flight.

Unmarked aerial hazards, power lines and poles, smashed buildings perfect for fouling the hoist, submerged cars, snipers, and panicked people rushing our swimmer or the basket. The entire city is an oil slick. The water is probably flammable, toxic at the very least and alive with the diseases from the sewers. The flood bottom is a jumbled reef of debris and sunken vehicles. There's not going to be a nice, easy, spot to set her down if something blows out. It will be a crash.

We lift off and turn west. One Three glides along easily. The storm is gone and the sky is clear. It's a beautiful day for flying. It is complete destruction below.

The tremendous force of the sea has scoured the coastline. Almost every attempt by humans to insinuate themselves on the edge of its realm has been smashed asunder. Their structures didn't stand a chance.

Mercy Flight

Once over the city, I can see other traffic all around us, but they're strangely small and distant, going their own way. I can't hear a damn thing in the headset, the roar of the One Three is too great, so I just unplug it. The city is gigantic, we're so small. It's a very lonely world.

But soon this world takes on some perspective, some direction. We land and load up on water. We're going to re-supply a hospital that's surrounded by the flood, cut off. Lt Bailey throttles up, the rotor blades take the strain and the whole airframe shudders. Lt Michael Rasch, our co-pilot starts pushing buttons and blinking lights. One Three puts her shoulder into it, I can feel her power now. The ride in part of things has ended. We're on station and we're going to do something about this situation. We're in the fight.

Bailey and Michael wing One Three low over the city. Everywhere I look there's disaster. Everywhere I look tiny people look up. Some wave, some just stare. The hospital comes into view, crowds milling around the grounds. We offload the water and onload people whose conditions can't wait any longer. Our rescue swimmer, Moises "Mo" Rivera, and our crew chief Karl Williams pack them in.

They load in an older lady who cries out in pain as we slide her up against the folded crew seats. Her knees are shot. Mo takes a head count and asks each person the particulars of their condition. Diabetes, kidney problems, heart conditions. The oldest man on board simply states, "I'm a WW2 veteran and I'm dying of cancer." Tears suddenly cloud my eyes. After all that, now this. It isn't fair.

Another man just stares mutely ahead. Type two Diabetes has left him nearly blind. One Three takes us over the city again and we leave them somewhere, the airport maybe, I can't remember. Ambulance people took them away and I never saw any of them again.

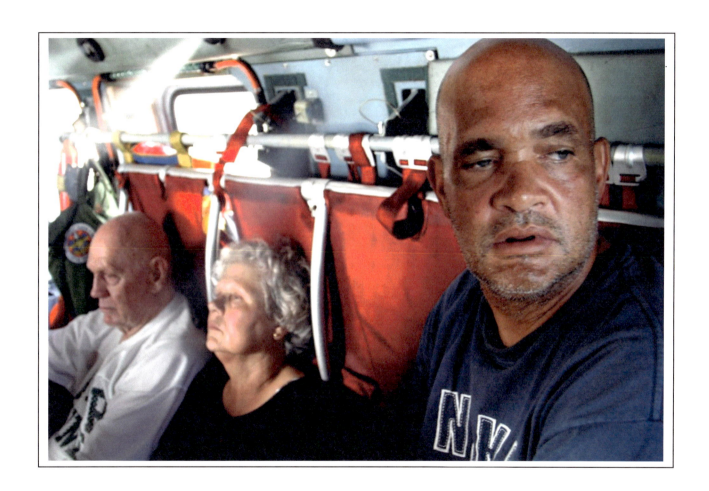

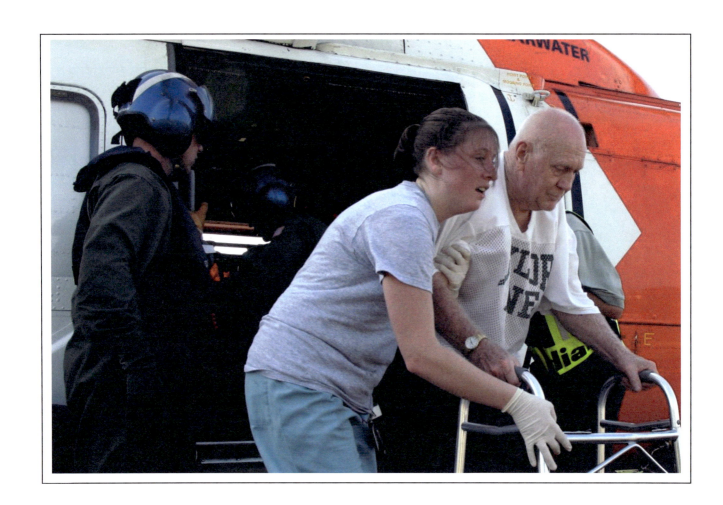

Crazy Day

After the hospital mission we flew to the Super Dome to land supplies and take out medical patients. After much dicking around it transpired that they had already been evacuated. This was a bitter pill as blade time on a helo is a precious commodity. Baily and Mike resolved that we would be doing what USCG birds do best…hoist operations. It was about to get really crazy.

We lifted off and winged back over the city. There was no shortage of people to rescue and we came in over a small group waving us down. Karl, the hoist operator and crew chief readied the basket and Mo hopped in. Down he went into the water and started loading the first person in the basket. Up he came and into the cabin while Baily and Mike held hover. Karl came around the basket and assisted the person out of it. It is cramped and that move was cumbersome. At one point it looked like he was going to fall out the open door. This wasn't going to work. As the next basket came up I yelled, "I got this! I'll handle the people!" He nodded.

I shoved the camera bag and extra gear behind some kind of rack and waited. The next basket came up and I helped the person out, asked if they were Ok and handed them a bottle of water while Karl kicked the basket back out. This was going to work much better and thus I became the fifth member of the crew, getting people out and placed with one hand, and shooting with the other. The hoist time was cut in half and from there on we were on fire. (a year or so later Mike told me that he had put together a lessons learned presentation and made the point that the extra crewman to fill that role was essential in a big rescue like this. It was adopted as policy.)

From there things got blurry. One after mission another, Mo goes down, Karl runs the hoist, I grab the people, we drop them off when we're full and on it went for hours. Eventually I had to piece together the whole day in my mind by referring back to the frames I shot. I had totally lost track of time and space.

Some memories stand out, however. At one point Karl was bringing the basket up and we heard these blood curdling screams getting closer and closer. I was like, "Wtf…?" when suddenly the basket popped up with two girls on board with their eyes closed and screaming their heads off. I got them out and put them up behind Mike, still screaming. "Hey! Hey!," I yelled. "Coast Guard, we got you, you're ok!" at which point they stopped, staring wide eyed around them. A moment later the basket came back up with their little brother on board. He must have been around ten. I got him over next to his sisters and yelled, "Tell me that wasn't really fun?!" He burst out in a huge grin, "Hell yea it was!"

Now, I could never see from my position who or what was in the basket as it was coming up so imagine my surprise when it popped in the door with a giant Mastiff and his owner. Everyone in the bird gasped. The dog looked around in near panic. He had just been lifted into the air by this giant, roaring insect and was now in its belly with strangers. I looked him in the eyes and yelled, "Puppy, you're ok! You gotta be cool!" He looked back with fear in his eyes but kind of nodded in his dog way, hopping out and throwing himself against me and would not budge. I stroked his neck and told him he was a good dog the whole way to the drop off point. When he and his owner got off he went a ways and turned back, jumped up and gave me a big sloppy Mastiff kiss. I kick myself to this day cause I didn't shoot a picture of them. A bunch of that happened. Busy I guess.

At another point we were setting up in a line of three helos who were picking people from an apartment complex. We watched one of the birds put their swimmer down on the wire and try to get to these two girls on a recessed balcony. They couldn't get him to them because of the recess so the crew chief started swinging the cable. On the third swing the swimmer reached over and just grabbed the first girl, snatching her like spider man as the winch sent them aloft. We could hear her screaming over the roar of the engines. He grabbed the next one in the same way. It was a bad ass move. The people we already had on our bird clapped.

We flew one mission to the top of some kind of school where a hundred or so people had gathered. Bailey and Mike scoped it out and came in even, between some power lines. God only knows how old the roof was so they held collective and power to keep 13 light on its wheels. Mo bailed out and spoke to some kind of leader who had emerged in the chaos. Only the folks with impending medical conditions. He had been ready for this and quickly pushed forward ten or so people. We got them loaded in and away we went. It was an extraordinary feat of flying. One gust, one wrong move and there could have been a catastrophe

But far and away the boldest mission was the old folks home. When everyone else had fled, two of the staff had stayed, moving residents by hand to the second floor as the water came up. They then went to the attic and chopped a hole through the roof and ceiling. Somehow they got word out and two birds were assigned. We came on station and send down the rescue swimmers. The situation was dire; very elderly, Alzheimer's, bed ridden. The staffers and swimmers set about widening the hole in the roof with rescue axes while Karl got the basket set up. Once it was sent down they threaded it through the roof and ceiling and we plucked the patients out one by one through the opening from the second floor. This was an extremely dangerous maneuver but they pulled it off, eventually taking out the entire group. There was no room on the bird so the two staffers said they would stay behind and flag down a boat.

This was the kind of courage I saw, time and again, all day. It just became routine. There was a job to do and people just dug in and did it. It was one of the most extraordinary things I've ever been party to.

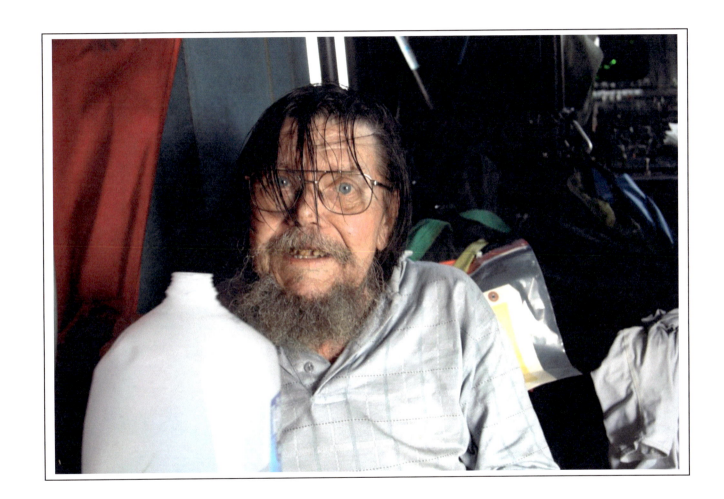

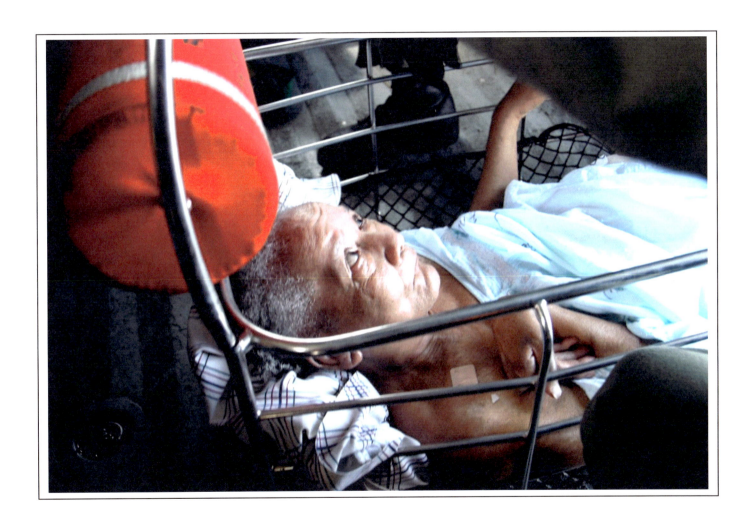

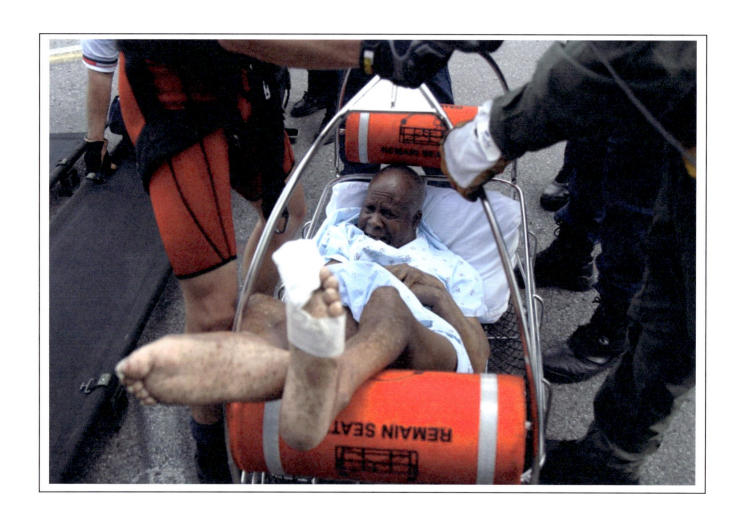

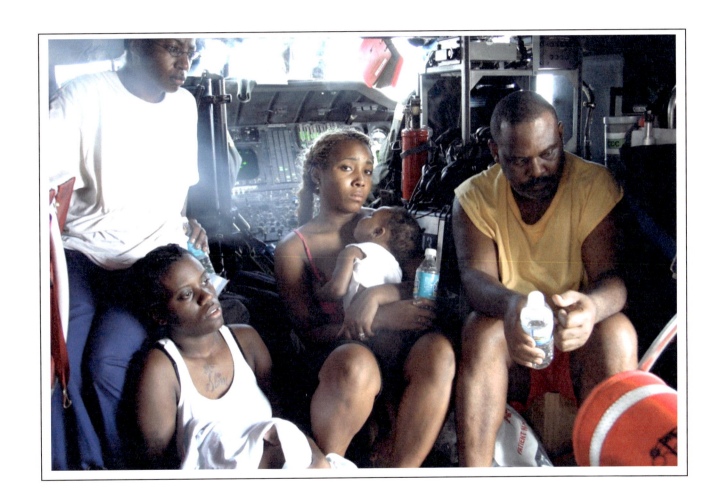

On the ground

I was lucky to have a very bright pilot who suggested I shoot the scene at the drop off point. As we descended with a load of survivors, Bailey told me he'd pick me up after a few loads. I hopped out and started shooting. It was here that the magnitude of this struck with full force.

Hundreds, thousands of people were pouring into the cloverleaf, disgorged by helicopters that seemed to stretch away for infinity. At one point I looked up and there were no less than 14 in the pattern. The roar of engines, the rotor wash, the intensity of all of it was staggering. It felt like something out of the fall of Saigon. People were coming off clutching small shopping bags stuffed with what few belongings they could grab, or nothing at all, swarming out of the city like rats off a sinking ship. It struck me hard that essentially these people were refugees, just as surely as if a war had driven them out, and they weren't going home anytime soon. Everything they had was lost. It was larger than anything I had seen in Bosnia or elsewhere. Tears welled up my eyes.

The drop off point was the cloverleaf where I-610 meets the I-10 interstate. There was a mixed mob of police, ambulance crews, and National Guard doing the hard and fast work of maintaining order, sorting, loading and sending people further up the evacuation chain. Lines of ambulances and school buses stretched out along the streets leading in. Those who needed medical went out on the ambos, those who could maintain went onto the buses. It was tense, fast moving and close to chaos. Somehow the responders were holding it together.

There was a makeshift field hospital set up under the overpass. They were overrun. The ambulance crews were working feverishly, but the heat was taking its toll. They brought one woman in, rushing to start fluids, but it was too late. She gave up a gurgle and died. They paused, and then turned back to the living, too many people, not enough time. I was struck by the thought that this is how it was for surgeons in a Civil War field hospital, hell my first tour in Bosnia on a bad day. But here they were wearing shorts and ball caps, surrounded by an ocean of empty, crushed plastic water bottles. The roar of helicopters was ceaseless.

Not ten feet away a small knot of National Guard MPs were getting people onto busses. The tension was high, people desperate to get out to anywhere but there. Many of them were not being very polite about it. These kids, 22yr old E-4s, didn't blink. They were firm and calm. I have no doubt whatsoever that their demeanor prevented a full scale riot. One by one I went to them and quietly said over their shoulders, "If no one has told you yet, you're working a miracle here today."

Wandering back to the landing zone I shot the helos coming in two by two. After a while I noticed that two of them were just hovering there, looking at me. I didn't understand until I realized that I still had on the big life vest thing and had the helicopter helmet over my arm. Wearing blue BDU pants and with that get up on and they apparently thought I was the ground control guy. Tag, you're it.

Lucky for me I know a thing or two about this stuff. Between the military, some flight school, and being pretty read up on helos (Chicken Hawk being the definitive work in this dept.). I knew that a couple things had to happen. First, they can't land simultaneously in that tight a space, especially in this mix if big and little birds. The one's rotor wash is likely to flip the one next to it. Second, there were several large street light poles that made for dangerous hazards. Would have to keep them off of those. And third, I need to sort this pattern out, they were coming and going in every direction. Good pilots all but this was a mid-air waiting to happen.

So I dumped the camera bag and the helmet by a guard rail and walked out further into the field. I made eye contact with both pilots, held up on fist to the Black Hawk while motioning the Dolphin to bring it in. I held the Black Hawk until the Dolphin was settled and powered down, and then brought him in. Then I brought in the Black Hawk. There I held them both until their cargo had made their way towards the road and were clear. Then I spun them back out in the order they had landed, motioning one to the north and the other south. The next chalk stacked up and we did it again.

There must be some kind of pilot telepathy, or maybe someone called it out over the radio that the LZ was now controlled. I don't know, but in short order we all were on the same page and things started really moving. Before long the pattern had fixed itself and they were lined up in two long columns that stretched back over the city. Again, I don't know if this was me, but it appeared to straighten out once I took control of landing and departure.

This went on for an hour or more. Every kind of helicopter in North America made its appearance. I saw 13 come and go twice, the last time Mike gestured they'd grab me on the next one. I grabbed a young cop who was nearby and said, "My ride is coming back. You see what I've been doing?" He nodded. "You keep this going, stagger 'em in and out, north and south. Next guy who relieves you, tell him the same."

Baily and Mike came back, I hopped on and we were gone again.

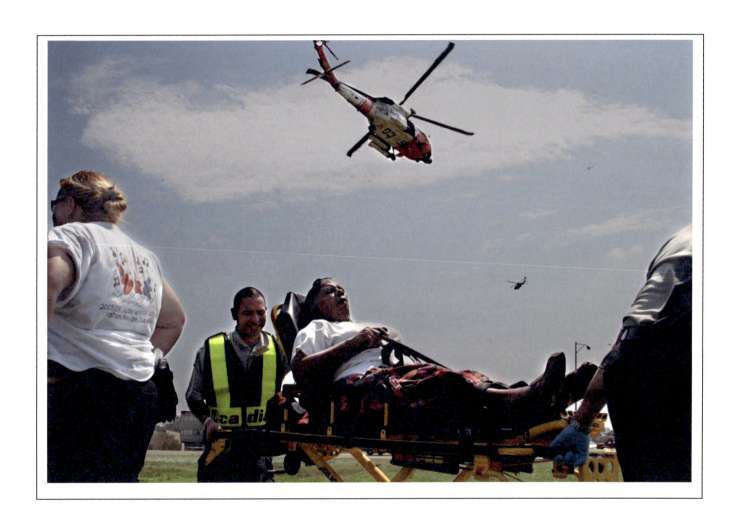

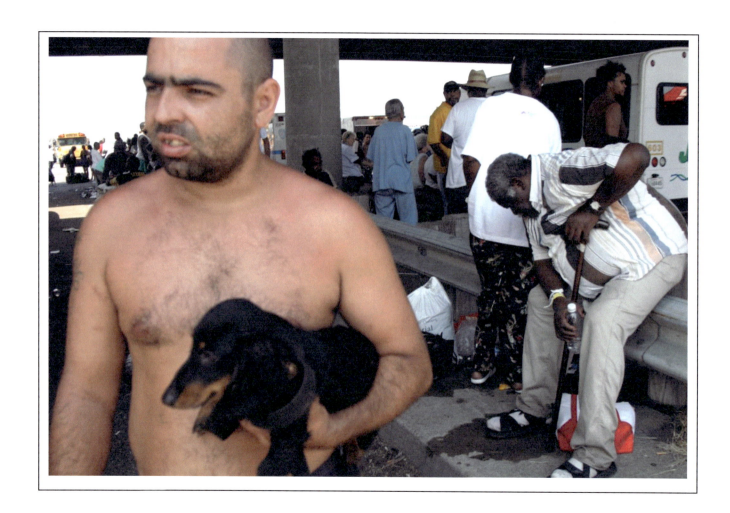

An American Dunkirk

After the air rescue adventure I pushed deeper into town and found the US Coast Guard and swarms of other boats hard at work. There were people from every agency and walk of life. Police, Fire, oil contractors, "Cajun Navy," US Coast Guard marine safety and aids to navigation units. Everyone who could float showed up and got to work. One guy, "Big River Billy," came from as far away as Taos, NM where he is a rafting guide on the upper Rio Grande. He just loaded up and drove down.

Many had been in the water since Tuesday morning after the storm struck, grabbing naps on the pavement of the onramps. The situation was far beyond anything anyone had previously trained for or experienced. They came to rescue people and on a few occasions got shot at. One crew from Illinois had started pulling survivors out on Tuesday only to have a riot break out at their drop point after the rescues looted a liquor store. A New Orleans cop pushed in and said, "Boys, this crowd's getting ready to turn on you, time to go."

When it became clear that they had an urban riot as well as a rescue on their hands, command started pushing in assets of a different nature. USCG law enforcement Maritime Interdiction Security Teams (MIST) arrived, bringing gear more appropriate to the situation. Rural cops who self-deployed with their bass boats added to the response. They brought some stability and things got rolling again.

The same hazards that faced the aircrews were there in spades for the boats, only worse, they were right down in the toxic water. You did what you could to stay out if it, but there was just so much you could do. There were people in there by the thousands and they needed to come out, so everyone just got to work.

Was it a bit chaotic? Sure, that's what happens when local leadership abandons their posts. Did the job get done anyway? Sure did, and it took no small measure of guts to do it. Hard information on the ground was hard to come by, rumors flew. Between the submerged cars, downed power poles, toxic water, and outbursts of violence this was a dangerous place to be. But it didn't stop anyone for long. They got in and got busy.

Again the days blurred, but some memories stand out. I ran into a man who had come down to the area we were working to help his friend find his mother. They got her out and continued dropping people at the on ramps. I made an admiring comment about what I assumed was his boat, but he informed me that he'd never seen it before. They had driven in as far as they could and spoken to the guy who was driving it. After over almost 18 hours out in the neighborhoods, he was so tired he was nodding off so he tossed the keys to them and wished everyone luck. Turned out that he had come by boat in the same way. No one had any idea who the real owner was; it had just been handed off to anyone who could get gas into it and make it go for almost four days. I saw it again the next day with someone else at the wheel.

A number of people I spoke to reported the same thing, people showing up with their boats and just handing them off when they couldn't go any farther. In fact, on Tuesday morning there was a line of private vessels stretching for almost two miles from where the water started on the 10 towards Causeway. A handful of firemen and a FEMA guy set it up so they could launch two at a time off the east bound side of the roadway and then return to drop their loads on the west bound side. It struck me as an American version of the evacuation at Dunkirk. Like that epic event it involved a whole lot of determination, ingenuity and went on for days.

Mixed in at one launch point was a large blue truck towing an airboat. Wearing a faded New Orleans police department uniform, this flinty-eyed old man looked like he probably had more than a few gunfights under his belt. He just looked like one of those mean old bastards ya don't fuk with. I don't think he said a word as he went about prepping the boat. We just nodded respectfully and mumbled "Sir," whenever he was near. He backed it down the ramp until the airboat floated free. Letting it drift, he pulled away, parked the truck and waded back to the boat clutching a black, evil looking Bennelli riot shotgun. The motor roared to life and he took off, crashing over and around obstacles until he disappeared down into the flooded neighborhood. A couple of weeks later, in photos, I noticed the name sewn on his shirt. "Det. P. Toye." Meeting a group of New Orleans police officers at a relief kitchen, I asked who he was. They pondered for a moment and then remembered that he had retired some years ago, long enough that these young cops didn't know him, only of him. My impression was correct, he was a legend in that department with many years of service. "Well, he wasn't retired that day," I said, telling them the story of the rattlesnake-eyed old cop with the airboat and a shotgun.

In midtown one morning I tagged along with the Maritime Safety Detachment. They put in their small boats and started pulling people out by the dozen. While we were there a lady paddled up in some kind of sailboat with a missing mast. She had found it floating around and piled her belongings and her dogs into it and floated around the neighborhood for a day or so. She found where we were loading out along some railroad tracks and came in. We got her unloaded and got the dogs some food and water. At some point she had come into a large cache of cigarettes. We didn't ask where from but gave her extra garbage bags to keep them in. Where she was headed, probably Houston, they would be as valuable as money.

The people I met who had been trapped by the waters had plenty of tales of their own, such as the firemen who had been trapped by the waters near the university campus; Engine 6, Ladder 3. After the storm had passed, their operational area was an island. They drove around where they could and soon encountered groups of residents struggling towards the high ground around the campus. They tried calling dispatchers but discovered that their radios wouldn't reach, the repeaters had been smashed down by the winds or gone offline from power outages. While they could hear the broken calls from police and fire units trapped in the city, their radios didn't have the power to push a signal out to anyone who would hear them. (In part, this inspired initial reports that police and fire fighters had abandoned their posts—headquarters couldn't hear their transmissions.) Engine 6 & Ladder 3 was going to be on their own.

Regrouping at the firehouse, they decided to set up on campus, where people continued to wade in from the flooded neighborhoods. No sooner had these groups begun to congregate on Monday afternoon than a helicopter swooped in and dropped off more people. (That early things had not been quite set up in the way I encountered when I went up with 13) At that point, any dry ground was better than a rooftop and the first wave of choppers were setting people down wherever they could in an effort to get people off the rooftops as fast as they could.

In short order, the numbers of people on campus had swelled into the hundreds. They were in need of every kind of supply, from clean water to diapers. With a truckload of tools specifically designed to break into buildings, the firemen breached a nearby supermarket and loaded up with water, food and mountains of baby supplies. Drafting a few good Samaritans and a handful of stranded UNO Campus Police from the crowd, they soon had a supply point up and running. While mass casualty events are a part of every fire department's training regimen, running a refugee camp isn't. They just drew on elements of their knowledge and common sense and were soon getting food and water to those who needed it.

But breaking into the supermarket turned out to be a double-edged sword. No sooner had they retrieved the basic necessities from inside than a mob descended on the place and began helping themselves to gallons and gallons of alcohol. As one might expect, arguments, scuffles and other misbehavior immediately broke out. As day one flowed into day three, the booze combined with desperation and anger and things started getting ugly. Rival, inner city gang members who had arrived aggravated the situation, making things even more dangerous for the firemen and the workaday people stranded there. In short order, the gangs helped themselves to women in the crowd, taking them away to rooms in the abandoned campus buildings. A typical case of the 10% idiot factor screwing things up for everyone else.

Eventually a squad of armed troops landed by helicopter and the firemen were relieved and sent to regroup and push back in as guides for the SAR boats. They hadn't really slept for over 72hrs when I met them but that wasn't holding them back. They were getting up and getting after it until the job was done.

On another run into town with the Aids to Navigation guys we encountered a group of guys who had ridden the storm out in a small, neighborhood bar. They told us they had slept on the pool tables when the water came up. They had blown through all the beer, most of the whiskey, and all the bar snacks. They didn't want to leave because they were afraid the place would get looted and they were water Cajuns anyway, so this wasn't that big a deal. Sooner or later, they felt, the water would go down. We gave them MREs to tide them over and I hooked them up with a pack of smokes, for which they were eternally grateful.

No small number chose to stay, especially pet owners when radio reports made it clear that little or no provision to shelter them or their animals had been set up ahead of time. (The Humane Society and SPCA would later address this) We went to visit a lady the guys in the bar had told us about who was staying with her dog in her upstairs rooms. She had heard on her battery powered radio about the initial chaos and was staying on until things settled down. She and her German shepherd Queenie were well stocked to sit tight until the initial rush was over. She sent word out with us to friends living up state so they could come and meet her somewhere in the coming days when it was all clear to come out.

And that's how it went for days. Go in, find a place to launch, get busy. Driving through stretches of water halfway up our car doors, I prayed aloud that the Jeep wouldn't flood out. This was not the place to be breaking down. At one point the Jeep actually started to float, a tense moment until the tires grabbed the ground again and it lurched itself up and out. God bless that truck. I still have it.

Few of the rescue contingents had ever laid eyes on one another before. Rescue crews came from Baton Rouge, New Orleans, St. Louis and other inland outposts in the middle of nowhere along rivers I had never heard of. But they were all there, all wearing the various colors of people who spend their lives helping people. FD, PD, USCG, EMT, ABCDEFG—all thrown together as if they were attending some strange convention where everyone refers to their clan by a series of letters. Didn't matter. Tie in, get busy.

The young enlisted kids that make up the backbone of the Coast Guard and other services were impressive. They went to work with a will, manhandling the flatboats off the trailers and into the water at every launch spot like kids tearing into their presents on Christmas morning. Well past sunset the little boats pulled people by the dozens from the neighborhoods and the drop points became a carnival of New Orleans society: black, white, Hispanic, artists, laborers, lawyers, homemakers, brokers, bakers, dogs, cats, everybody. The kids went out until the boats were full, landed everyone, and then went back out for more. They'd assess the condition of each of the rescued as best they could, making sure everybody had water or first aid. When a neighborhood was clear the kids just slid a few blocks down and started in again. There was no let up.

Any contention that the rescue was delayed by anything other than security concerns, was selective, or biased in any way is pure bullshit. No one held back for anything other than gunfire or riot. The rescue fleet, from all walks, went into extremely dangerous waters and worked with a will, out of the gate. I saw it with my own eyes, day after day. Anything to the contrary is a damn lie.

"Big River" Billy Miller.

So I met Billy on one of the many on ramps the boats were working out of. He had an airboat, we talked, took a spin to go pick some people up and talked some more.

Billy is a river guide out of Taos, NM who lives in a converted school bus. He saw what was happening and decided to head down. He had a heavy duty 13 man raft that might be useful. So he loaded the raft and his brother in the truck and off they went, from New Mexico to New Orleans.

Somewhere along the way he spotted an airboat for sale on the side of the road. He pulls in, cuts a deal, leaves the raft, hooks on and keeps rolling. He doesn't have a clear picture of how this is going to roll when he gets there, but drives on anyway.

He rolls into town and sees a line of trailers and slides into it. The next thing he knows there's a cop directing him to put the boat in. He does, parks the truck, fires it up and roars out into the city. There's only one problem…Billy has never driven an airboat in his life. Next thing you know he and some poor souls from 9th Ward are bouncing the thing off submerged cars and fences, and at one point almost get flipped over by the rotor wash of an Army Chinook helicopter.

But Billy's a sharp guy and quickly masters the thing, carrying god knows how many people to safety throughout the week and ferrying a crew from ITN around. As things do, the operation came to an end and Billy drove the boat out of the city.

On the way he saw a dump truck for sale on the side of the road. He pulled in, cut a deal and spent the next two years helping the people of NOLA dig out the debris.

He is one of the coolest people I have ever known and we have remained friends ever since.

He went on to invent a pontoon airboat that has set all kinds of speed records, running across oceans, rocks, and ice. Extraordinary guy with a huge heart.

Doing the Math

What never seemed to be conveyed effectively on the news channels was just how much material and logistics goes into an operation of this size. There is no such thing as magically descending from the sky and yanking people out of a disaster area.

For example, in the sort of heat present in the New Orleans area at that time of year, basic life support for a single person requires at a minimum 2 gallons of clean water per day. With the municipal water supply completely offline that meant it had to come in by truck.

2 gallons per 10,000 people per day = 20,000 gallons at 8lbs per gallon = 160,000 lbs of water per day. That's 80 short tons per day. For a million that's 100 short tons per day. The average army truck can carry 5 tons. That's 20 trucks of nothing but water per day for only 10,000 people.

Mind you that that just covers what you need to simply stay alive. If you're stressed or moving around, working, double that. Then add on basic hygiene and sanitation and you're approaching a national average of over 100 gallons a day for a basic family of four. That's 250,000 gallons per day, weighing 2,000,000 lbs that has to be trucked in across a road net in shambles.

We haven't even touched on food and water for the rescue personnel, fuel consumption for their vehicles, shelter, gas for generators for communications, spare parts for broken vehicles, man hours for maintenance, etc. The list grows and grows exponentially by the day. Hours fly by trying to get all of that into the area across a broken infrastructure and into a city under water.

The hue and cry from the media about the speed of the operation was baseless. We pulled it off in 7 days. Every person in need of shelter, clean water and food got to that place. It started on the on-ramps and went all the way to the Astrodome. 7 days. No one else could have done that.

Epilogue

Even after all these years, the evacuation of New Orleans remains the most intense and moving experience I have ever been involved in. Sarajevo, Baghdad, Russia, and all the other crazy places I've gotten myself into all had their moments and their own flavor. But for sheer intensity and scope of human drama, nothing comes close to NOLA.

In the months after the storm, they fixed the levee issue, cleared the debris, and slowly brought the town back to life. I have been back a couple times. It's a rough town, it's a musical town, it's a flavorful town. There is no other place like it on earth. But there's two towns now…the NOLA pre-Katrina and the one post-Katrina. Lots of people never came back. For some it presented a chance at a new life and they took it. Lots of people died, taking their own unique flavor away from the neighborhoods they lived in.

But lots of people stayed, and new people have come to town. There's a strange blend between the old and the new, a transition where the Delta Blues of old are blending into the digital hip of today. It's been bumpy by some accounts. But realistically, when hasn't it been that way in NOLA? Hard as it can be, it's part of the flavor of that town. That's why the music and art are as pure as they are. You need pressure, and heat, and humidity, and struggle to make that kind of art. NOLA has it still.

It took a long while to process everything I saw and did. The first version of this book was part of that. The other was jumping into Myspace and linking up with others who were there, a big group share. One was a musician named Brian "Rooble" Rueb. He posted pics of his destroyed vintage guitar and amp collection. I wrote and told him about my musician friends from Sarajevo who had lost everything too. The guitars were replaced and the music sustained them. He was going to make it too. Last I saw on Facebook he had a bunch of gigs lined up. NOLA Lives on.

About the Author

Writer, photographer, storm chaser, and First Responder. Jim Bartlett covered international conflicts, disasters and disruptive events since 1992 when he left the US and traveled as a freelancer to the Former Yugoslavia.

Arriving at the Zagreb train station in the spring of '92, he fell in with diverse elements of the Croatian army and soon found himself in Northern Bosnia. Amidst the chaos of that conflict, where he became resident for the majority of it, he developed a deeply personal style and platform for storytelling not often seen in the mainstream.

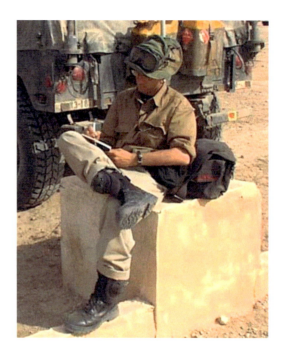

In 1996, he helped launch the internet age by becoming the first war correspondent in history to be based entirely online. His news blog, Berserkistan, co-produced with Emmy winner Michael Linder, cultivated a readership of 155,000 across 33 countries. That was pretty impressive in the days of 56k modems.

It was to be the first of multiple conflicts he covered, from Brcko to Baghdad, in a variety of media, from print and photo to TV. His byline eventually appeared in everything from Esquire to Soldier of Fortune.

In later years he drifted into the world of first responders, becoming an AEMT and Wilderness Medic. Today you can find him kicking around a rescue squad, a forest fire, or a shady venue with local musicians. For those who risk it, life has flavor the sheltered never know.

Made in the USA
Columbia, SC
09 November 2024

45803730R00055